in the bird
museum

Acknowledgements

The poems in this collection have appeared previously in *Adroitly Placed Word, Alice Blue, Agni, Backwards City Review, Caffeine Destiny, Columbia Poetry Review, Cranky, DIAGRAM, 42 Opus, Ink & Ashes, Kaleidowhirl, Melic Review, Milk Magazine, PFS Post, Poetry Daily, Poetry Super Highway, Rhino, Seven Corners, Sharkforum, Slipstream, Siren, Swink, The Tiny, Tryst,* and *27 Rue de Fleures.*

Several pieces also appeared in earlier versions in chapbooks, including *feign* (New Michigan Press, 2007) and *brief history of girl as match* (dusie chap kollektiv, 2007), as well as several self-published volumes.

Special thanks to the journals, readers, and fellow writers who have supported, published, read, and critiqued the work herein, and to Susana and Dusie for publishing it. Also, to the visual artists who inspire me, the writers whose work I love beyond reason, and the poets I've no doubt stolen stuff from (you know who you are.) Finally, to my family and friends for their support, patience, and all manner of other good things, without which this book wouldn't have been possible. --KB

ISBN 978-0-615-25686-3

in the bird museum was typeset by the editor and set in Gills San and Adobe Garamond.

First Printing, Kristy Bowen 2008

Dusie Press Books

: Dusie Press : Zürich, Switzerland :
: editor@dusie.org: www.dusie.org :

in the bird museum

kristy bowen

Dusie Press Books, 2008

CONTENTS

I.

II.

III.

IV.

V.

VI.

...I had a terror--since September--I could tell to none--
and so I sing, as the Boy does by the Burying Ground--
because I am afraid- *Emily Dickinson*

I.

a short history of the corset

Note the necessity of small hands, keyholes.
A dilation of the eyes, the haunted cabinet.

Like in dancing:
lift the torso from the hips like an egg
from an egg cup, and let the chest
lead as if being drawn forwards
by an upward pulling string.

Taken from the latin, corps,
but then all nouns are accidental.
All grammar, merely chance.

We understand
no more than a pale lick of skin
beneath bone, the sighs
of cloakrooms or lilacs.

While hardly fit for bird calling or orchards,
the body requires correction, the borders defined.

See how easily one could slip outside of a story.
Even through a locked door, quietly.

a few precepts of convention

Even sewing can be suggestive. Or envelopes, the sigh of folded paper. Letters sliding into dark spaces. Remember, a young girl unprotected by a chaperone is in the position precisely of an unarmed traveler alone among wolves.

To be out of the house late at night, or sitting up, except to study, are imprudences she cannot allow herself. Surely someone will note whom she receives, at what hour they go. Take, for instance, the virgins in the back room, spines bent over their arithmetic. Even their milk teeth are orderly.

A young girl must not, even with white sandals or blood oranges, go on a journey that can by any possibility last overnight. To go out with him in a small boat, or violet skirt, seems harmless enough, but might result in a questionable situation if they're becalmed or left helpless in a fog. Once, a man and a girl went out from Bar Harbor and encountering a still blue, did not get back until the next day. To the end of time, her reputation will suffer for the experience.

application for the melville dewey school

Bindings:

Materials needed:

awl, book cloth, box board, bamboo skewer, bricks, linen
thread, beeswax, book press, brush, wooden boards, bone
folder, needle

Do you, or have you ever?

when I said ruined,
when we say shuttered
we open our throats to lemons.
Not a shiver, but a trespass, first
the halving, then the miscarriage.

Instructions:

If the signatures are falling apart, perform the brittle paper test:
  a. fold the corner of a middle page back and forth two
     times, then pull.
  b. If the corner comes off easily, the paper is considered
     brittle.
  c. If the paper is brittle, the book is a candidate for a box.

Cataloguing:

Hair color: _____
Measurements: _____
Marital Status: _____

At the carousel, there was a tumbling, and then, a door.
The skirted tables, bare legs being known to provoke.
Also, her penchant for reckless dresses.

in his "Brief Rules for Library Handwriting"

[to] take great pains to have all writing uniform in size,
blackness of lines, slant, spacing and forms of letters ... [and
to] follow the library hand forms of all letters, avoiding any
ornament, flourish, or lines not necessary to the letter." (1)

Analysis:

The writer's attempt to maintain a vertical slant reflects her
effort to adopt a detached or impersonal attitude, positively
characterized by independence and restraint, but negatively
by self-centeredness and rigidity. This aloof and impartial
demeanor, reinforced by wide spacing between lines, reveals
someone resisting the influence of both outside forces and
inner emotions, preferring to rely on reason. The potential for
cruelty is evident in the blunt endings of many downstrokes or
counterstrokes.   Prone to various afflictions, not withstanding
debt, or fevers, or disorders of the mouth. A pause between
the letter "s" and the letter it follows indicates a love of foul
weather.

the dollmaker's apprentice,
or various form of violence

Now that we have capsized
in our dark boats, the milk

goes bad, incandescent.
Still, he loves them, pale

invertebrate things, how they
suffer of astonishment,

of pinafores. The heart
like a hinge box,

or better, leeches in a jar.
We went out in the glass-bottomed

boat and upset the teacups.
Night gathered like a skirt.

On some subcontinent, we broke
the spine of the thing we could

not name. The tiny woman bathed
in blue light, who wanted

an umbrella, wanted a suitcase,
needs a dictionary, and only

the smallest lamp.

an essay on the constellations and other messier objects

Moreover, we delight in concealment,
the similarity of satin to stain.
The page torn along the diagonal.

At breakfast, the daughters are immaculate,
sepia-voiced. Look at their failures,
their hairpins, their ability to balance an egg
on end for hours. The atlas becomes
a telescope. See how small their hands,
all points leading to the hyphen.

Now, desire haunts the milk pail, the radium bleed.
They cut away, they loosen. Note the multitude
of variables regarding stability:

index, line, the weight of carbon.

rules for irregular nouns

1. genus, genera

    a. Forget the thing you came for. as in:
            There are trees enough between us.

    b. Syntax breaks all the bones ,
        fashions an index or an acanthus.
        Remember:
            I was threadbare and calm, and the splinter still
            inside me.

    c. Here, we came for the ghost of the word
        inside the other word:
            When seen at a nervous distance,
            the leaves that spring from her mouth
            resemble sparrows.

2. nebula, nebulae

    a.   Beware any direct object that ends in –ment. It commonly implies slowness and pralines.

    b.   One word may possibly be confused for another. As in, the instruments were very accurate the dark gears, incredibly precise.

    c. Like diagnosis or phenomenon, many are remnants of archaic systems, (Germanic, Indo/European, et al.)   You believe her when she tells you the radius of her palm equals the width of a star.

3. stratum, strata

    a. The tongue prefers the Latinate, the celestrina and the castanet.

    b. She was holding a nest of paper wasps,
        the window sills covered with silk.

practical uses for table linen

At night, someone rearranges the rooms
in my body, pushes ottomans into

corners and hides the water lily print.
Now, I'm all reckless stairwells

and falling sounds. Entire bedroom sets
gone missing at sunrise. You're fondest

of the shifting windows, the ivory boned
sofa shaped like a woman's back;

have placed buttons beneath carpets
and hidden pens in all the closets.

The parlors fill with pink paper
dresses and impossible chairs.

The kitchens, understandably, hide their knives.

mr. godey's latin

i. what x equals

mother, mater, maternal
two, duo, dual, duet
tooth, dens, stem. dent, dental
foot, pes, stem. ped, pedal
heart, cor, stem. cord, cordial

ii. that which sings to the thing that sings in her mouth

a. the poet is giving the girl large roses
      (or is giving large roses to the girl)
b. the girl is giving the poet's roses to the sailors
      (or is giving the sailors the poet's roses)
c. without money, the girl has nothing
      (the courage of the girl is not strong)

iii. the arithmetic of dresses

a. fortuna derives from fors--chance, accident, the girl saves the poets life.
b. without philosophy, fortune and man often go astray
c. we often see the penalty of anger

fret

Lets say a woman's heart
is like a wind-up bird.
The conservatory filled
with oranges and the cellar
disordered, unstable
with the pull of thieves

gathering outside the windows.
I've invented this: the panic,
copper tongued and shaken.
I'm dizzied, dulcet.
A thin layer of graphite
blooming beneath my skin.

And here, my slight of hand,
my tour de force,
skirts come all undone
and tapping out code beneath
the dressing table. I am
impossibly lovely, impossibly
fixed against the horizon.
Any attempt at flight
ruining all the furniture.

from the dream concordance

pg. 67   you were thinking torn and the
              hyacinths had teeth

pg 78   caught when telling a lie, her teeth began
              to crumble into her palm

pg 89   an atlas roughly the size of a table, his teeth
              gleamed in the lamplight

pg 99   forgotten the buckets, milk-heavy, the day's
              teeth already into her

pg 104   the space behind her teeth and
              tongue purpling and erratic

pg 107   when bending at the waist, the movement
              of the comb's teeth along the scalp

pg 110   hard toothlike projection from the beak of
              embryonic birds, assists in hatching, and
              later falls off

pg 112   the top of the backbone and already in the
              teeth, the fever spreads to the ears

pg 130   exhibited a certain sweet tooth and affinity
              for layer cake

pg 145   loss of teeth could denote a deprivation of
              vitamins, but may indicate a loss of love. Unusually
              large teeth may indicate dishonesty or
              wordiness.

from the hysteria notebooks: a gothic

1. Catherine, for a moment, was motionless with horror.

Our story indicates the parlor door
remain closed, the lace at her wrist
worn, and slightly rent. Granted,
there are bones in the body science

hasn't even discovered yet: this,
the one at her throat that tightens
when the pale dress takes flight
from the window, or the slivers
in the ear discerning motion.

He had then proceeded to throw suspicion upon the girl,
saying that he had heard from Frau K. that she took no
interest in any other thing but sexual matters, and that she
used to read Mantegazza's Physiology of Love and books of
that sort in their house on the lake. It was most likely, he had
added, that she had been over excited by such reading and had
merely "fancied" the whole scene she had described.

II.   Attitudes Passionelles

When he touched her, violets on her tongue, and afterward, in
the folds of her bed linen.

Landscape plays a greater role than one would think . The
dark moors, the moon. How can we but forgive this girl, dear
reader; her dresses unravel us. Or him, his penchant for the
distraught. Now, we are moving through dark rooms, the rustle
of skirts, held breath. Something must have been here in the
moments before, the thread that, alas, saves us disappearing
round the corner.

III.   Rest Cure

Hippocrates first proposed
that hysteria was caused by a
wandering uterus. He believed
that the uterus could dislodge
itself in the body and wander
around
the female body attaching itself
to other organs. He explained
that the various symptoms of
hysteria, such as nervousness,
depression, and hysterical fits
were caused by the uterus's
interactions with the other
organs in the body.

You see, the woman in the attic is nothing
more than the axis on which our heroine turns—
countryside, silver locket, cover of snow.
A bread knife has more to do with it than how
many saints she could name in one breath.
Here, an illustration.

Take away the books. The sharpened point
of a compass, its circle widening. We are apt
to fear the body, the sentences scrawled beneath
the teacup's pale lip. Each tendon a wire,
jumping at the proximity of silks.

The villain is you father. The villain is your doctor.
The villain is your mother, ten years gone
and wearing white. Once they've taken
away the paint box, you can stop pretending.
 Those darling, fragile reds.

four answers to one question

arrangements

Note the correlation between the altitude
and the ribs of her silky continent,
the hinge and pivot in the hips
that falls prey to perimeter.
The point at which the tongue
becomes accustomed to corruption.

specifications

Seldom do we see so many fractured
discoveries, the wreck of branches,
the armful of nettles. A bottle
hangs by a string at the bottom of a well,
translucent and perfected. I was apprenticed
to the frenzied atmosphere, the verandas
that open into dark wind.

axis

A woman frequents the solar flares now,
with her tiny fusebox and basket of pears.
Collects feathers and dowses the surface
for a vein of river cool and pristine as
the word for snow. Mercurial, she would
say, of imprecise origin.

interference

There's a danger in railings, mailboxes,
anything with the barest hint of longing.
We suffer along grander dimensions
than this, the muscles
that twitch electric each time
we remember cold.

instructions for the young naturalist

Meanwhile, in the deep shade, the body's lit interior,
the idea of soft is given. He prefers me like this—
ghosted, afflicted. How the language candles
to the windows of the cabin, rattles the cyclamen.

This is how the sky is hung. I open my mouth
and the throat remembers at which point the water
takes to cold, that the blackest bird survives
overnight despite us. Because it is fractured.

Because it is tilted.

excerpts from Mme. Charlotte's Flower Dictionary

azalea: typically denotes temperance. As children, we peered between the pale ribs of the porch. The ache of laundered sheets, the sweep of hair.

columbine: folly, or interrogation. The opposite of primrose (consistency). Indicates a love of small bodied things and dressing for dinner. Her stationary sported irises (meaning message) to make matters more complicated. What are we trying to tell?

holly: foresight. A girl in love with water, how she hums to cisterns, fisted in her tight bed.

lavender: distrust. the opposite of violets (faith). Perhaps affiliated with the slipknot. The scrim. Her uncle's model of the cosmos.

marigolds: sorrow. We are enthralled with our own heaviness. The birches stretch pale arms, while fossils line the shelves of the study, the unlit lamps, the boxes filled with wings.

rhododendron: danger. I've been dreaming witches again. Women bent over beds of perennials, laced inside the latticed windows.

zinnia: absence, or merely aperture.

index, or list of devices

II.

at the hotel andromeda

we walk up the stairs, walk down.
Put too much sugar in the coffee.

Button, unbutton.
It's all very hush, hush.

Like the beginning of a play
where we take out the dishes,

put them away, or the death scene
where the scenery tears at the edges.

He coaxes us with cokes and marbles.
The penny voyeur, his marionette,

the hot pink hibiscus of her mouth.
Shows me a drawing of a house.

Then a house with birds.
A dovecote, a broken key.

I take out the stars then put them away.

classifications

Not the bird, but merely the picture of a bird,
and I'm all wound, all wound.

Pensive, pale, pirouetting
in sequins and feathers.
Losing my passport on the train
and inventing my name.

Your seance gives me the shakes,
little eggs quivering carnivorous
in my palm.

I'm a shipwreck in a bottle,
full steam. The part of the painting
where the painting has been taken away.

The balcony. The woman in the boat.
All I know about mathematics:

that it makes a pretty bride, makes a pretty mess.

untitled (bebe marie)

There is something of the accidental,
the eye of the collector, inadvertent

and endeared to the small, odd gift.
Perhaps I was anchored

and the lanterns lit my limbs
like dried sticks, deciduous

and prone to tiny thrushes
lining the rungs of my ribs.

Now all the dresses are worn
and unwashed, their hems dwindling

to floss, and something to be said
of obsession, this locked box,

the voices rattling the glass.
I was a footnote,

a honey comb.
I was the muddy bottom beneath the ruin.

The point at which all the objects
rename themselves,

their tiny imaginary lives.

in the bird museum

It's all glassy eyes
and glued feathers.
Canned song leaking
from the speakers
and up the stairs
to where we sleep.

By definition, my mother
has beautiful hands.
By definition, an excellent
range of octaves.

Even her washcloths taste
clean and damp and faintly
like soap. Even our zippers go
up and down without snagging.

My sister breaks a parakeet
in half and it unravels like a spool
of twine in her hands. Dissolves
into springs and cotton batting.

The song is a trick of logic.
Of the ear. We'll wrap it
dishtowels. Pray for a
good rain, a good shovel.

toward the blue peninsula

Say we make it out intact.
You, with your moths flickering

in their tiny jar. Me, with this terrible
ocean between my bones.

Are we then haunting or haunted?
And is it always like this--

the feeling that someone
has just left the room?

Was I sighing or coughing
when the wire gave way

and the door opened?
Were you speaking?

In Spain, I have a friend
who makes the tiniest paper boats.

rescind

In the story in which Amelia
is transformed into a dozen sparrows,
day arrives like a rustling in the mailbox.
A chalky, soft bodied sighing.

Dressing her, we are seized by
the mechanics of it, counterweights
shifting and clamoring against her spine.

Her pronouns are off for days.
She becomes you becomes it.
We make a hole in the house
big enough for whatever arrives
still breathing, torn open.

The irony is in the stitches
we use to make things whole
again. The damage that
touches the wires touching.

in the night theatre

there are far too many entrances
and exits. The girls who love
black shoes and vodka come and go
in the blue light, hiking up their skirts
and running their fingers along the edge
of the butter dish. They are easily subdued,
seduced by surgical pins and shards of bottle glass.
Now we'd call them nervy, a piece.
Insect-like, they collect more than their
weight in fishing line, tangles of silver
tinsel. Bent over the baby with a globe
for its head, its body a jar of watch parts,
they don't feel a thing when the lights go out.
Don't feel a thing when it's emptied.

experiment in miniature

As always, I'm devastated by that shade
of blue. The hint of hotel rooms
and anything French. Tend to fall
for the short notes, the staccato.
This seasick vibrato, like the girl
that opened her mouth so wide
you could hear the wind inside.
Her wreckage of trees and wheel spokes.
One dance card, then another.

No one loves a brushfire, or worse,
a dirty blonde. The grotto with a thousand
bones rinsed so clean it was erotic.
You might carry them home in your pockets
like birds with tiny marbles for eyes,
newspaper where their wings should be.
Might cut their tongues out.
might name them for your own.

III.

feign

Here, all the girls have small bones.
The smallest. A languor of yellow
scarves and spelling bees.

The day gives things names and we
hide them between our thighs,
beneath our mother's mattress.

We make nice with the books, with the dishes,
with the men behind the blue shed.
The ones lurking in the bus-stop woods,

crouching near water heaters in dark basements.
I can lie clean through my white teeth.
My white dress round my waist

and my panties in the bushes.
To be expected, there are
the usual accidents on train tracks,

in third floor bathrooms.
Nothing can be assumed.
I was a mouth and worry came to me.

I was gingered and soft like a pear.

trouble

The girls you love make beautiful suicides,
breaking off heels and losing orchid
corsages beneath the backseats of buicks.

This one speaks through the curtain
of her hair, the sweet blonde number,
soft machine of her ribs humming

like an engine block full of bees.
The dark has too much rigging. The moon
projected on a screen with tinfoil stars.

Is full of holes. Bankrupt gas stations
and the backs of women's calves.
Your flares set fire to the homecoming float.

Set fire to the gym and all its paper
carnations. All the mouths gone metallic pink,
harboring tire irons and rhinestone tiaras.

brief history of girl as match

In the blue house, we are
coat rack and clutter.
Safety pins and antibiotic ointment.
Prone to night sweats and inflourescence.
The frayed ends of power cords.

I dismantle the piano first,
the back storm door.
Am obsessed with simple machines,
giddy with typewriters and transmissions.
Air conditioners. Electric mixers.

Can go for days like this sometimes,
smelling like lemons and diesel.
Dress made of paper,
I burn like nothing you've seen.

girls reading novels

Violet is named for lavender equations, the glitter at the end of
your spine. Avenues grow contradictory, the length of chain-
link divided by the waters' murky circle. Kitchen floors tilt at
a seventy degree angle while intricate societies are discovered
among the broken dishes. My limbs are symmetrical, polite.
Ask me a question and I answer by rubbing the rim of a
drinking glass. See, how I 'm stitched : the dark fabric of sky,
the body torn from petticoats and corsets. The cuts all have
names. Dawn and Olivia are favorites among the killers just
now emerging from the bushes. The faucet drains its litany of
bathrooms with dark webbed corners and we forget the name
for sky, the discordant hum of tendons wrapping the twilight.
There's a name for the door that opens into the darkened
hallway. Some terrible violence in the way I say open.

final night at the sunset drive-in

And what else to do with a girl
with a mouth like a dirty book,
a burnt-out car. Blue limbs

tangling the windshield and every-
thing tilted and still. This isn't a porno,
it's a love story--tongues everywhere

and desultory lines. A woman on
the screen keens like a broken radio.
This one tastes like americana,

the burnished chrome of dashboard
instruments. Flip-flopped coat-check girl,
her skirt fussy and florid, over her face.

Her breath, all orange crush and flicker.

saints

Now, the saint of fingers through hair,
of imperfect engines. Paper gone pink
at the edges and the whiskey-throated

woman finished singing. Saint of fifth
grade valentines crumpling in desks.
Of mouths pressed to palms

inside sleeping bags. Of chairs
and sevens and the dark seats
of movie houses. Saint of imaginary

tables in lengthening rooms,
of aqueducts and porcelain cup handles.
Of lanterns in trees and the all the kitchens

on fire. Saint of the beautifully
drowned. Of yawns and picnic tables.
Backseats and trailer parks.
Soap and tequila.

O' saint of irregular seams.

the paper house

At the edge of the field, we see the angriest
bodies. The spell is in the wrists. The spell, in
the shampoo. Girls with long throats and a
penchant for divining rods. In the end, the
house burns beneath the moon opening like a
mouth torn out of a book. All our rooms have
wants, our wants, broken doors. We smolder
beneath dresses. Our buttons, our brocade
dark. Even now, the mice shred newspapers in
attics filled with cages ripped from hooks in
parlor walls. In parlors ripped from a woman's
skin, all eyelets and hooks. At the edge of the
field, we watched with matches in our skirts.

girls against boys

When she makes an o of her mouth,
the forsythia behind her head bursts into flame.
Singes clotheslines full of blue gingham
pinafores and yellow flowered sheets.
When she bends at the waist, she can make an o
of her body. A birdcall. A tiny pink sequin.

Can make up names for the baby teeth
beneath her dresser. Lydia. Amelia.
Their tiny lion tin. Can define the pinwheel
of her arms falling through dark.

The trellis by the steps slicks in the rain
and all night he calls for his extra rib,
his good heart's hinge. No one can sleep
with it. The world, all checked
cotton and charm bracelets by now.
Every verb imperfect.

midnight pastoral

Suppose we could describe it: the bird collector
with his binoculars and net gone home to his wife

in her blue-lit kitchen. The black pot boiling over on the stove
and the goats outside rubbing their bodies against the fence.

Who knows what he cages or what survives the night.
A girl in a white dress arcs toward the dark horizon, the world so

small you could climb out of it. So small you could pocket
the moon with a cupped palm. Suppose we could describe

her movement through bluestem and aster, or describe dress,
or girl, or even sky. That beautiful black climbing.

According to the birds. According to the goats.

instabilities

All along, we'd thought we were in love with weather.
Azaleas blooming inky against the fence and all

the porch lights loosening. Women named Alice
or Ingrid smoked in clamorous rooms with long windows,

their spines opening to back roads and folksongs.
We thought ourselves in love with thirst, whether

or not the sky opened and showed us its teeth.
We dreamt of beheadings and antebellum skirts,

power lines crossing and re-crossing the atmosphere,
frenzied as the letters of our names.

isabel of the wreckage

Too much iron in the soil and the grass
won't grow. Impatiens falter, swelter
in the dusty kettle. Too much metal in the water
and doors swell in their frames. Spoons bend
backwards and the kitchen smells of fever.

Sediment in the iced tea, and a girl begins
to see things. Bluish shadows peeking
from beneath quilts. Flies gathering at her hem.
Yesterday, she bled through three dresses.
Pinwheel heart and lockjaw. Even the bodies
pulled from rivers are woundless, immaculate.
Rinsed clean as the bones of old pickups,
the ghosted acres of tires.

Door to door, amnesiacs wander in the low hum.
The collision of their bodies sparks brushfires.
Pallid tongues move from mouth to mouth,
unzipped, their breath scissored and alum.

our lady of anemia

She begins with tiny spoons and screws.
Swallows safety pins and penny nails
by the dozen. Paperclips, thumbtacks,
salt shaker tops. The doctors say its
dire, prescribe lithium and fresh air. Her
mother cries and brings cake. Last week,
they pulled a watch from her stomach,
still ticking. Wrapped her tight in white,
wet sheets until her skin grew soft,
amphibious. Every morning is clear and
bright. Every morning she spits dimes
into the sink. Her nightgowns, drafty,
ravaged by openings. After all, a girl has
too many holes as it is. Things are bound
to fall through once in a while.

spectra

The distraction could be mistaken
for a chair, the moon for
a frantic dress. Not a woman
pulled from water, but an image
of her, what we invent based on light:

If angle of refraction (r) is related
to the angle of incidence (i),
how long before the dressers
empty of her clothes? We agree
sun is burning through the clouds,
but have no language for it.

What startles, we grow accustomed to:
this irregular blue, or the pitch
of red that invites murders in houses.
Now, I can say, maybe this happened,
and the retina shifts its rods and cones,
makes it so.

sarah leaves the midwest

Never the black water rippling, or the road signs bent by wind. Not the anchors, or the underpass, or the bridges. Seldom the difficult swimming. Canals dragged for bodies every spring. Or the tentative gravel parking lots, their tires filled with paper wasps. Not the splinters in her mouth or the spangles in her hair, blue as the inside of the virgin. Rarely what we call interruption, neighborhood dogs in their dusty ghetto, their wilderness of bed sheets. Scarcely the stained saucers and rusted spoons, or this block, and all the houses catching fire. Never again the emptied dresses, frozen to the grass, or cavities in her teeth, humming.

another cautionary tale

This one begins with girls,
candied and small boned as mice.
Begins in kitchens or hallways.

On the phone or in cars beneath picnic
blankets. When the killer comes
from the bushes. From the closet.

From the backseat of a blue Cadillac.
The girls line up like a seam. Fight back.
Fashion a rope from their hair, a compass

from a compact. When their date goes
for gas, they stab the psycho with a nail file,
hide the evidence beneath pink twin sets.

Harbor something black and lush as licorice
beneath their tongues. Swallow the man
with the hook, the stranger inside the house.

When left alone, poison the boyfriend
and bury him beneath the cellar. Slaughter
the narrative, read it backwards like the gospel.

The dirty, dirty word in their mouth.

iv.

prologue: the haunting of archer avenue

For the most part it's all true:
the white dress and fade. Radio
static and the street slicked black

as cats. Ask her where the light goes
and she'll say dancehalls, their music
dwindling to a note that silks along

the inner ear. But here, she's
an understudy of dark, the slip
in the shadow that speaks

like a girl, but isn't. Kiss her
and she tastes like broken light bulbs.
Batteries draining in parking lots.

Doubt inhabits the space between cars,
the drag of headlights over grass
just thickening in the cold. Imagine,

if you will, the pitch between stoplights.
Kiss her and the landscape swerves left.

Invocation

Sweet Mary of the ballroom, the rum punch and sly grin.
Mary of open car doors, cold spots. Fox trot, slow dance.
Mary of the table knock. Mary of pick-ups, blue lights, and
power lines. Threadbare Mary. Truck-stop Mary. Mary of the
culverts. Dance hall, car crash, borrowed dress. Blue eyed
Mary. Bloody Mary at the end of the bar and gasoline Mary.
Tavern chill and black sedan Mary. Mary of the gearshift, Mary
of the burn. Abandoned Skylark and parking lot Mary. Mary
of the argument, the dark stumble. Trailer park, cakewalk,
charmschool Mary. Mary of hair ribbons and the unhinged.
Cartwheel and kolatchke Mary. Mary of the big bands, tire
ruts, screen doors. Lipstick and jitterbug. Mended hem and
ankle turn. Apostrophe Mary. Catastrophe Mary. Mary at the
edges.

the way it happens

He meets her in a bar or along the road. It's raining. Snowing. He has a blue coat. A yearning. A father with the silence and all. A friend of a friend. It happened. He didn't see her come in. Asked for a dance. Asked for directions. It's always like this. The distance and the tiny purse. The jazz and the dizzy light. Earlier, the gin fizz. The giggle. He tells a lie. His mother is dead. Or his wife won't listen. She places a hand on his wrist. Against his cheek. The road is always slick. The snow comes early or it doesn't. He drives with one hand on the wheel. One hand on the mirror. On her thigh or her throat. She's distracted. Lives nearby or close enough. When he kisses her. When he leaves her at the gate. When they approach the cemetery, she disappears. She cries. She sets the car on fire. Sets off on her own. Walks right through the gate. It was late and he doesn't remember. It was dark and her dress was stained. Things like this happen all the time. Her mother is a thin woman with a Polish face. Her mother is dark-eyed and heavy. When he knocks on the door. When he hesitates at the gate. When he returns the sweater left in the backseat. He's shown a lock of yellow hair. A photo. A girl in a prom dress. She's smiling or she isn't. Been gone for years. Just a month. It happened in December. It happened in June. She liked dancing, or smoking, or cussing. She was a flirt. Or fast. Or too shy for her own good. It happened here, or somewhere else downtown. Outside the cemetery or in the parking lot dark. There was a fight and a swerve and the wind knocked out of her. There was a wreck. A tree or a truck. Her name was Anna. Her name was Maria. Her friends called her Mary. No one remembers. She was buried in an unmarked grave. In her ball gown. Or something orchid, tea length. It was all over the papers. I read it myself. Her parents moved away and never spoke of it. Her date swore he went looking for her. Swore he was never on that road. Swore he never saw it coming.

the luxury of borrowed dresses

She'd gone near dizzy in the dressing
room. All capelet sleeves and velvet piping.
Shoes akimbo and gathered tulle fuzzing
the chandeliers. Much too cold for organza
anyway. The crème chiffon. The bias silk.
And this fringe, so last year. Her friends
glittered and glossed as pearl pocketbooks.
And her, slipping into each gown like some other life.
This one with enough flounce to forget her mother
sewing buttons, French ones, for 5 cents a bit.
To forget the shop girls. Their sad, tidy lunches.

burn

The tail light put the dark
in her mouth, this rubied gleam.

Black lake beneath her nightgown
littered with sparklers and roman

candles. At home, the stockyard filth
in her mother's kitchen sullies

the mended bedspreads. The bleached
bones of peaches. She breathes

a little sometimes. Swallows a silver
locket lifted from the thrift store.

Not the real girl with the dress
rehearsal and the geometry of sixes.

But the one gone musty in the throat.
Gone deep in the milk white.

the vanishing hitchhiker: a study

You see, the limbs are accidental. Riddled by vagueness and blue-checked aprons. Her back arcs against the seat and the sweet black mouth of the soprano opens and opens again. The myth delineates her leavings and arrivings. The dirty books hidden beneath her bed, her lips red-dark and unruly. When you inquire after her address, she offers a taxonomy of saints. Spreads her thighs and shows you her phobias. The creeper vine at her throat won't let her sing anymore, but she'll gesture erratically. Offer assorted sundries, hotel soap and chewing gum. Her eyes like lemon cake behind the glass. Sugared and untouched.

the graveyards of chicago

You can see our lawns are lovely.
Their fences precise. No shoddy stones
or wilting gardenias. See how well
the steel mill provides. The highway.
The misstep and tidy sickness.
Our angels line up row by row.
Almost god. Or close to it.
And ghosts? No ghosts.
Only nightshift gin and kids
fucking in the bushes.
See how our marble shines.
Even the pigeons love the dead.
The vernacular of plots and greening.

st. andrews day

Once the house has emptied
of its birds, the water holds
the shape of her. Buckets,

bathtubs. A landscape of rusted
locks and falling brooms.
She counts fourteen fence posts

and finds a knothole big enough
for her wrist. Melts the Sunday
candles in her mother's best

kettle and still nothing.
Last night Ava and Anna
must have hidden the red scarf

beneath the breakfront.
The husband game, and each
of them a ribbon, a rosary.

Nothing under her plate but its shadow.

roadside inventory

The ribs are a lovely museum, you know. All spooks and
idling Chevrolets. Amazing the glow that finds its way into
open spaces. This mouth like a broken reflector, a length
of silver chain. I've carved a heart in the tar that lines the
shoulder and assembled my name in bottlecaps. In ditches,
the discarded tires resemble murders. Slender pickets of
crosses lingering at their margins. There's a racket in the
things left behind. Each name a handbag or a hairpin. The
forked heat of backseats. My limbs are riddled with sisters
lurching along interstates. Their pink shoes abandoned at
the turn. How they all lie down like this. Lie down like
this. Lie down like this.

last call

In the parking lot, all
the dancers are lovely
and drunk. Symmetrical.

Kissing in the blue dark.
A girl pins a tiger lily
to her shoulder, itches

beneath silk. Comes
closest with the boy
who still smells of his mother's

laundry soap. Still opens
his mouth to her like a door.
When the yellow of her dress

singes against the spotlight;
when she heaves into the
hydrangeas, he still loves her.

Everything glittered
and moving through violet.

justice, illinois

Maybe the landscape holds them,
water on three sides and the dead
too many to count. A profusion
of clotheslines and baseball diamonds.
How the streetlights dim as the third
shift kicks in.

The waitress at the diner
has no tongue but says enough
with her eyes, her beautiful limbs.
Maybe her dreams are treeless.
Every car wreck a broken cassette
tape rattling in her trunk. Every
ghost expected.

Her husband keeps
a roadkill deer in the freezer,
hits her only when he needs to.
Calls his mother little bird.
The telephone poles have her name
all over them, the foxglove grown
over in the ditch.

There's nothing you can say to her that
doesn't sound like breaking.

the imagined lives of ghosts

Perhaps they are, after all, godless.
Licking the finials and mothering
strange black dogs. The boxwoods
alone accumulate thousands,
precarious as jukebox lovesongs.
All of them enamored with objects.
In love with birthday cake and
the backs of stamps. See how they
rhyme in couplets, how their
shoes don't match their skirts.
And velvet. Yes, velvet.
As if any of us have enough.
As if the low-watt gleam
of silver guardrails doesn't charm us.
How even the road bends to meet them.

swerve

I am bending toward the headlights
when the sound goes out. One minute
the wind in my throat, my hair,
and the next nothing. I had three sisters,
I tell you, and each of them a china figurine.
A man, he took my sweater and gave me drink.
Took my keys. Took my name down in a book
and offered to drive me home. I can't stop
these headaches. The jagged glass beneath my
tongue. I wear my quiet like a charm bracelet
tinkling at my wrist. This body practically
a crime scene by now, all dusted and closed.
My sisters cry and make wreaths. You wouldn't
believe how hot my hands are right now.
How tiny my fingers.

midnight at chet's melody lounge

Again, I dream I've killed you.
The back of your dress taking on
rain and the windows fogging over.
I dream a radio and a bedroom.
I dream a button and a bead.
Someone who looks like you
but more like me, moaning
into the backseat.

We both smell like sugar and wax.
Both trace our names against the glass.
Like sisters. Only better.
Bless us for our mothers.
For the yellow hair dyed black.
For the rum in our cokes
that makes us lovelier.
This thing that burns behind us
grown fierce and clumsy as our fingers.

V.

bibliophobia

fear of books

It begins with auguries. Three starlings. Three forks. The faucets running milk in the mornings and my handwriting hinting at some impending disaster. I'll speak in third person when we come to the part in the play where the house is on fire. The part in the car where my ribcage blooms like poppies. Where we die, are revived, then die again. Where the terror is exquisite. A slow, beautiful throttle.

dysticaphobia

fear of accidents

When the villains come for us,
even the basins are filled with
honey. With laudanum. The low
hum of pink satin. In the pantry,
we're sick with them, our limbs
thick with sawdust, moths rattling
the screen where the night gets
in. Just yesterday, three girls fell
from a tree bruised and ruined. A
commotion of hands at the wreck
of their dresses unfurling in the
dirt. Now we're fevered, fervent.
Even the latched things unlatched
and prone to disaster.

hydrophobia

fear of water

While we sleep, the river takes the house like a thief. Like a woman with a mad scene, a bad streak. Smashing all the windows and leaving bluegill in the sink. I gutter every light, wring the dark from my dress, heavy with lures and the tiniest blue snails. Every syllable rescued from the dank cellar of my throat. Something ruined and bone white as the bottom of boats. Virulent as the thickening ditches. Every girl gone crooked with summer. With the cattails and terrible light.

electrophobia

fear of electricity

After we've lined the shoes beneath
the bed, we fashion a makeshift radio,
duct taped, out of Dixie cups. Splinters
in the palms of my hands, current in the
baseboards. A woman sheds her clothes in
the kitchen and I have pinned a carnation
to my breast, to all the blue dresses lilting
on the lawn in that twilight, the streetlights
flickering. A scar where you wrote it in my
book, the blood part. Where I'm rusted.
Borrowed. A turn table with a broken arm.

lyssophobia

fear of madness

These things rarely turn out well. Always the tripwire. The small door in the wall. Teeth marks on the broom handle. The endless burlesque of babies and buttons. Everything red and red and red. The women are half-alive with loosening, the sweet smell of kitchen gas or car exhaust. Crazy with the rooms expanding inside their lungs. The slow shriek of teakettles. The dark parts. The hide, then the reveal.

chronomentrophobia

fear of clocks

By the time the moon looks like a broken watch, we've emptied ourselves of want. The linen napkins having flown into the hair of a girl shaped like a cake All pout and vanilla icing. There's a swelter to my vowels these days. To yours. Heady, like red wine. Silt gathering at our ankles, lining our dark pockets. In the bone black trees our limbs are still lovely, still lit by low watt bulbs. So much wicker. So much camphor. We're swimming in it. Embryonic and prone to the slightest pink. My shadow is a woman holding a lantern and a globe. She singes. Sings.

arithmaphobia

fear of numbers

Ten o'clock and I'm lit, livid with gin, in love
with the alchemist and his cheekbones.
His wife that drops like a coin into my
glass. Her dizzy fizz. Ten and I'm counting
pencils in the space between the bed
and the floor. Where I live on licorice,
the whirl of ballerinas swooning on vinyl.
Where I live on the palest underside of
their wrists, the 1/2 beat, the port de
bras. Where I've chewed all the dark out
with my crooked mouth, my gleaming arc.

erythrophobia

fear of red

Sometimes, it was all red. The dash light, my dress, the fire alarm of my mouth. Even my hair makes a sound like that now. Before you know it, I'm the patron saint of disaster. Of car crashes and open hydrants. The vowels gone round and sloppy in my mouth as candy. For luck, I carry three vermillion birds in the bottom of my purse. A cross in the crux of my crimson bra. In the furnace of my lungs, sometimes there's a hissing,   a swirl, like a sink emptying. I am careful not to riot.

ornithophobia

fear of birds

In the end, it's the gothic that gets us, sets me folding and unfolding like a note pinned to a dead girl's sweater. I take away the curtains. The pale cages. All that's left are the rabbit gloves and the doves that appear, unwilled, beneath the bed one by one. The catastrophe. The burnt out mouth of me. Tongueless, I was paper white, present tense. Heavy with vertigo and a violet nightdress. Moving my arms around to stop the room from filling with wings. My throat opening and opening.

VI.

footnotes to a history of desire

---

[1]   a woman who believed her voice was kept in a jewelry box locked in her mother's bedroom.

[2]   I placed the blue vase on the mantle, then smashed it the morning. Tiny white porcelain doves mocked me from the sideboard. From the tree outside. Dirty, dirty, they said.

[3]   In the short film "Diary of Eleanor," a girl folds her body down and down like a letter until she is the size of a pin. Her lover does not recognize her among the contents of his pocket. a spool of twine, a packet of seeds. She is lost indefinitely.

[4] Oddness, oddity:

    1.The quality of being odd (ODD a. 2) or uneven; unevenness of number.

    †2. Uniqueness, rarity, singularity. Obs.

    3. Divergence from what is ordinary or usual; strangeness, peculiarity; eccentricity.

[5] occurs in the dream in which she is rescued from the trees by an army of swallows.

[6] Adropogon gerardii, or big bluestem.   A variety of tall grasses prevalent in the upper Midwest., often growings in such tall, dense stands that it prevents other grasses from growing around it by shading them out.

[7] In Greek mythology, Philomel was loved by her sister Procne's husband, Tereus, who raped her, cut out her tongue, and held her captive. She wove a tapestry informing her sister of her fate, who in revenge, killed their son Itys and fed him to his father secretly. Tereus tried to kill both sisters until Zeus changed them into birds.

[8] "god in the machine"

[9] sometimes referred to as la porte de follie {sic} a door leading to an enormous room filled with plastic birds. See Darwin's Orgin of Species, Book I.

[10] Extravagant, or excessive., as in pretentious, reckless, ridiculous, silly.

algorithms

If Wednesday, then x = suggestion.   y will equal the lit
interior of cars, the distance between bodies. In the bath, if
the surface tension breaks at exactly 88 degrees, then y =
fragment , but only if the hands shake. If windows, then rooms
without objects. If objects, then x will be roughly equal to the
distance between the wrist and collarbone, but divided by the
circumference of a plate. Assume a broken pitcher of milk, a
gesture. If your ribs ache, then subtract the body's weight in
water, or better, deduct your mothers age when you were
born. In bed, y always equals mouth. On Sundays, x can equal
religion, but can also equal canaries. Yesterday, x = envelope.
x + y occasionally equals daughter, but only when mothers are
present. x will nearly always equal hands then, or compass.

the synaesthete's love poem

Yesterday, blue tasted like licorice.
Even wind chimes caused dizziness;

an ache of paper lanterns rotting
from the acacias. Perhaps the L

in my name makes you sad,
evokes a film where a woman

waves from a train. Or how
this horizon wants to be a hymn.

If you listen, you can
hear the holes in the alphabet,

sounds lit by the lamps
of our bones. Perhaps

with this page I could fashion
a boat or a very convincing window.

A dress made entirely of vowels.

how to read this poem

I suggest a system. A lifeboat. Or at the very least a bathtub.

I suggest you sit down.

I suggest the bird at your shoulder be ruby-throated with a milky eye. That it say inappropriate things at inappropriate times.

I suggest bringing something ruined. Or broken. Or drunk.

I suggest you take the south road. Slip beneath the piano and out the trap door. Sneak up on it from behind.

I suggest you take a snack. An umbrella. A dictionary.

I suggest you start slowly.

I suggest you read the red skirt as a metaphor for sex. The fistful of poppies languishing in their vase.

I suggest everything is a metaphor for sex. Even the bird.

I suggest you mind the foil, toiling in the background. It's all very Shakespearean. Even her red hair, Shakespearean.

I suggest you take the setting into consideration. Or here, where the narrative slips off its track.

I suggest you look askance when the woman opens her arms and lowers them.

I suggest you be kind. But distracted.

the migrations

Once again, I am somehow wearing
the wrong dress for this dream, carrying
a jar with its feather and spool

of light blue thread. I walk from one house
to another where he deerflies gather
on the water's black back, mosquitoes

thickening beneath the pines. Say
I'm a girl in love with latitude, the tiny

birds that make their way to the lake bed,
winter at the muddy bottom.
Say my skin smells of dirt and heat.

Yesterday, the ornithologist's wife
carried five eggs in a metal bucket
twenty miles in her bare feet to tell you this:

One day, we'll fly in a perfect line.

instructions for when traveling abroad

Nonetheless, a flashlight is indispensable. Beware the winded,
or plundered, or spilled. You never know when bonelessness
may prevent accident, particularly when dancing with Italian
men.

On every continent, obscurity invents mystery. Chewing gum
may help. A petticoat beneath a black skirt may mend the
interstices
between syllables. Be prepared.

For every vaulted ceiling, or tattered manuscript, draw an x
across your forearm. Do not long to steal the chandelier or
place
oranges at the foot of St. Cecelia.

On Saturdays, wash your lingerie in white, scentless soap.

sleeping sickness

Soon, all your poems have trains.
Lurid, erotic places plagued

by vagueness and mangroves. Still
the sunlight undresses the terrain,

opens its bones, its throat, and
even oranges begin to fever you,

the white slip sweated to silver
and the tea gone tepid

in its pink rimmed cup.
You want something scenic

and disastrous, the dearest thing
stolen from the king and plied with honey

until her irises bloomed like grapes.
How insomnia recalls pennies,

white cakes in pretty boxes.
Even the sheets rinsed in lemon water

and gathered beneath the half moon.

the unhappiness of objects

From this vantage, there's an
indication of hotel soap and

window boxes. Two keys sewn
into the hem of my skirt and a flurry

of birds to the left of your hand.
My given name is a revision,

a bicycle at the bottom
of a lake. Here,

where guitars swell with water,
make intermittent advances

toward tune. Where we rub
two stones together and hope

for rain, the sky laundered
to a light grey.

letter to my art deco lover

Sadly, we are all angles and geometrics.
Nothing fits. Me and my backhanded,
back-roomed speakeasy of a mouth,

my terracotta limbs. Swoon me
and I faint from a balcony into pure
black lacquer and red velvet chairs.

No room for ghosts with everything
so symmetrical. Your machine gathers
heat in the basement beneath women

hanging their stockings in pink-tiled
bathrooms, smoking long cigarettes
and hiding behind their hair. It's erotic,

the perpendicularity of stone and
hotel lobbies. Gin-soaked, even the
broken elevator makes me hot.

bossa nova for the new bride

Sometimes, even the octaves are dangerous.
Notes just low enough to set you spinning.

A barbed question mark at the base
of your spine. All kitch and dangling hooks.

In the kitchen, the amnesiacs will be beautiful.
Even the suicides, beautiful.

You were waiting in your plastic coat
for the lemon-yellow dresses, feet together

like a girl in a movie. O, the space you
took up unbearable. Crossing out

the names with a felt-tip pen.
Breeding canaries in the bureau

and lusting after broken things.
All that splitting and sewing.

All that carnage just waiting to happen.

entropy

The night the windows all crash
in their frames, I'm not the shambled

aftermath or the boy-girl order.
Spaces between us are not spaces

at all but a thousand blue flowered
nightgowns. You haven't yet learned

to discern the shape of things according
to your tongue. Heavy cumulous hang

the sky like sheets from a line
and entire alphabets go missing.

In the dark, a woman's teeth
flicker on and off. We'll decide

who's leaving by scientific method
and the rule of light bulbs and iceboxes.

My skin allows enough lumen for boxwoods to glow.

lake effect

And after all the guessing, plastic castles
and ballerina flats, you still open your seams

to the world like a good little shipwreck.
Sometimes the sun is a compass, sometimes

a burning barge. They dismantle the shoreline
and a thousand years go missing. These men

with their lenses and tripods. With their discontent
and their mouths opening. They climb inside

with flashlights —seek the voice box, that rusted
bucket, where ribs tighten and ghostfish

swim the pale lungs. Perhaps your hearing is off,
and when they say ruin you

can't stop thinking of rain. How, sometimes
the water wants to be a blue door.

Sometimes the girl moving toward.

A poet and artist, Kristy Bowen is the author of *the fever almanac* (Ghost Road Press, 2006) as well as several chapbooks, including *feign* (New Michigan Press, 2007) and *at the hotel andromeda* (with Lauren Levato), a book art project inspired by the work of Joseph Cornell. Her book, *girl show* is forthcoming from *Ghost Road Press* in 2009. Bowen is the editor of the online poetry zine, *wicked alice*, and founder of *dancing girl press & studio*, which publishes chapbooks by female poets and offers a selection of book, paper, ephemera, and vintage inspired arts & crafts in her online shop, *dulcet*. Born in 1974 in Illinois, she possesses an undergraduate degree in English and Theater Arts from Rockford College, as well as an M.A. in Literature from DePaul University, with an emphasis in women's writing and feminist criticism. She recently completed her MFA studies in Poetry at Columbia College. Her passions include Joseph Cornell, victoriana, carnival sideshows, horror films, diagramatic things,

archives, old scientific & botanical illustrations, architectural drawings, postcards, and all things paper. She lives and writes in Chicago in a big old art deco building near the lake, where she funds her writing and other (mis)adventures by working in the library of an arts college. Her work has appeared in electronic and print journals like *Cranky, DIAGRAM, Agni, Rhino, Slipstream, Backwards City, Caffeine Destiny,* and *others.*